I0755976

FINISHING LINE PRESS
www.finishinglinepress.com

The Forager's Exit
Bee Centos

poems by

Victoria Anderson

Finishing Line Press
Georgetown, Kentucky

The Forager's Exit
Bee Centos

ISBN 979-8-89990-382-3 First Edition

ACKNOWLEDGMENTS

Banyan Review Issue 19:Fall 2024
"Hive," "Forager's Exit," "Swarm Psalm," "The Emptying," and "The Hem of the Story."

Publisher: Leah Huete de Maines
Editor: Christen Kincaid
Cover Art: Medieval Beekeeping, Hives and Bees, Tacuinum Sanitatis
Author Photo: Mark DeLancey
Cover Design: Elizabeth Maines McCleavy

Order online: www.finishinglinepress.com
also available on amazon.com

Author inquiries and mail orders:
Finishing Line Press
PO Box 1626
Georgetown, Kentucky 40324
USA

Contents

Near, nearer, all the way
to the bedside of the dying world.
Diane Suess

How the body, the landscape, finds one
vibration and for awhile, hums
Aaron Baker

My Mouth was Wax, My Mouth was Honey

during such days
of path and vein
stone or vision
something wordless
and near

the humming circle
flowers with lemon
stained throats

always in the arms
of something
always swaddled

when I reach the hive
bees cluster
a pulse of light
rises in song

Love and Honey

On the field of early rye
 and yarrow light,
        the hive.

Inside a tangible vibrancy,
        a reminder that the world
        offers unknown goodness.

A lesson in unlearning,
        utterances translatable
        without language.

Just occluded presence
        cleaved of meaning,

just the seethe of coiled energy,
        encoded.

Hive

an ill-lit hostelry
           silked and hollowed

entrusted to the hour
           of animals' quiet churning,

of the deeper
corridors of mystery

dark untellables
these angels of nothing
                     these small, plural things

Past the Field of Shifting Greens

the nest built of sonics
          murmuring traceries
                    bees clustered

inside their god cage
          in the everything flows
                    steady go of the world

Opening the Hive

foreseen   enterable
          the limen world
                    hushed & glittered
spelled out
          with the finest nib
                    letters too small to read

Dark Hum

no proceeding from
          no gnawing through

the hatch enchambered
          inside our imaginings

dark and viewless
          as they are

Hexagonal

into the blouse of roses
        little wings scattered

into the bank of hum
        the brood sealed in wax

inside the hive
        queendom itself

and somewhere near
        a soundless flash, a hazy swath

Flight

Throbs to the earlobes,
skitters the morning,
sparkless into grooves,
sings in your green mind
stunned, singed, brightened.

In the Small Hour Gaze

map the noises
        the fine damp grass
                a green rampage

the tufts of yellow blossoming
        a garden of dark shapes turning
                curbing hard & away

across the stanzas of air
        a pulse of light coiled in its cell
                a lion-colored day

Forager's Exit

hived: shrined: vesseled
          cells swelling
                    a strange   unutterable music

in the dark center
          a shifting: seismic
                    an exit: wide and loose
                              a god's mouth unfastened

a tilt towards the throats
          of wild blossoms:
                    shrines to their own longing

Feral

through feral space
          sounds ricocheted
                    outside of language
                              tumbling out at us
                    like smoke
          which is to say
mostly gone

The Emptying

light's
unforgiving
reveal

A diminishing fugue
an intricate ballet
of leaving

headlong
into the muted world
into the crevices between
world and not world

the ruin fresh
some minor god's
instrument broken

Swarm

In the museum of bees, there are no bees
Mark Wunderlich

A mad shiver
then a wilding

the hive subtracts itself
in layers

a deep release,
a sigh.

Like prayers,
they leave

their cavities
and rise

into the garden
of broken fruit

dark shapes turning
tumbling out

A hush fringes
the night

renders the house
resonant.

Swarming Season

The most mutable among us
opened their wings
and stepped out
what remains is various:
a gold, lengthening flame,
a faint chorus of desire,
a door from the world,
its tilt and meander.

Tremor Path

disappearing things
looping out of the known
into the deepening
corridors of mystery

angels of nothing
traceries
curling into the wild
& spiraling dark

Swarm Psalm

a burnished ripple
          swells and goes flat
                    a song unfastens

shrine to their urge
          urge and nothing but

god glitter in our minds
          divinity enough
                    this wholeness finishing

Fissure

the hive scatters
its pulse waking the sky
with stanzas and staves

all certainties desert:
the bursting world
now fringed with loss

the folds of the year rustle
& trace the ragged line
to shape the weight

of a world pulled apart

The Sting is no Sting

Wildflowers electrified
in lizarding grass
the cost of entering a song
of unleashing
its sweetest wrongs

The Queen's Lament

A dollop here, a mess of particles there,
a dance no one dares anymore.
The narrative got punctured
and some of you are dead.

I have sat on the shelf called wife
but it was melancholia, late
and last in the soon.

I was made by being apart
where all the love-dead
live and breathe.

Besotted with interiors,
I carry the hive within.

The Hem of the Story

Little gods trying out their wings
          harmonize in silence
                    cannot be held by my gaze.

I follow the clues
          past the flowers dilating,
                    past the leaves, under their sheen.

Some have flown past death,
          radiant beings urging every kind
                    but my own.

Vigil

the dead we carry
          survive in distant heavens
                    having curled into the wild

on wings not burning
          but aflame
                    light its own truth song

Cento Sources

John Ashbery, Jabari Asim, Elizabeth Alexander, Mary Jo Bang, Ellen Bass, Gabrielle Bates, Anne Carson, Cathy Linh Che, Franny Choi, Hart Crane, Olena Kalytiak Davis, Maggie Dietz, Natalie Eilbert, Lisa Fishman, Forrest Gander, Linda Greger, Linda Gregg, Aracelis Gimway, Leslie Harrison, Seamus Heaney, Sara Elizabeth Johnson, Bridgit Pageen Kelly, Donika Kelly, Yusef Komunyakaa, Ada Limon, Maggie Miller, Jenny Molberg, Mary Oliver, Jill Osier, Nathaniel Perry, Paisley Redkdal, Jo Shapcott, Mary Szybist, Tracy Smith, Ocean Vuong, C.D. Wright, Jenny Xie, Dean Young

Victoria Anderson is a Chicago writer. She received her doctorate in American literature with a creative writing concentration from Binghamton University, New York, and has published three books of poetry: *This Country or That, Vorticity,* and *The Hour Box*. She has been published in numerousliterary journals, including *(b) OINK, Mississippi Review, Gulf Coast, Atlanta Review, AGNI, American Short Fiction,* and *Berkeley Fiction Review*. She is a three-time recipient of the Individual Artist Grant from Illinois Arts Council, and has had residencies at Ragdale and the Virginia Center for the Creative Arts. Victoria is retired from Loyola University Chicago, where she taught poetry and directed the Writing Program. She divides her time between Chicago, where she writes, and Michigan, where she keeps bees.

www.ingramcontent.com/pod-product-compliance
Lightning Source LLC
LaVergne TN
LVHW090542110826
845146LV00003B/1230

* 9 7 9 8 8 9 9 9 0 3 8 2 3 *